Beneath Stars Long Extinct

Beneath Stars Long Extinct

poems by

Ron Egatz

Red Hen Press | *Pasadena, CA*

Book design by Mark E. Cull
Book layout by Sydney Nichols

Cover art: "La Passeggiata, Positano" by Julie Jones Ivey
www.juliejonesiveyphotography.com
Author photo by Baldomero Fernandez
www.baldomero.com

Library of Congress Cataloging-in-Publication Data

Egatz, Ron.
  Beneath stars long extinct : poems / by Ron Egatz. — 1st ed.
    p. cm.
  ISBN 978-1-59709-486-3
  I. Title.
  PS3605.G37B46 2010
  811'.6—dc22

                              2010008021

The Annenberg Foundation, the James Irvine Foundation, the Los Angeles County Arts Commission, and the National Endowment for the Arts partially support Red Hen Press.

First Edition

Published by Red Hen Press
Pasadena, CA
www.redhen.org

Acknowledgements

Among the many writers I've been fortunate to call my friends, the following individuals have been most supportive of my own writing and generous with their expertise and time: Dick Allen, Laure-Anne Bosselaar, Françoise Brodsky, Kurt Brown, Mark Cox, Tom Disch, Stuart Dischell, Stephen Dobyns, Brooks Haxton, Thomas Lux, Dean Parkin, and Kevin Pilkington. The authors and past and present staff of Camber Press have been a constant source of knowledge, pedagogy, and a pleasure to work with. Special thanks to Frank Virgintino for friendship, talent, and support. Love and thanks to my comrade David Biedny for many years of deep groking, tasty tones, and unceasing truth.

Some of these poems have been previously published in the following publications: *Cimarron Review, Berkeley Poetry Review, Georgetown Review, Greensboro Review, Glimmer Train, Washington Square Review, Oberon, Smiths Knoll,* and *Washington Square Review.* "Into First" appeared in the anthology *Never Before: Poems About First Experiences,* edited by Laure-Anne Bosselaar.

Multiple articles in the *New York Times* were the sources for "First Motor Vehicle Fatality in America" and "Airline Stowaways."

James Langford told me the story which starts off "Box of Ash."

Thanks to Marika Brussel for fact checking and so much more on the poem "The One."

Contents

Love and Otherwise

Number Eight,

for Jenn.

Even the stars up in the sky look a mess.
—Werner Herzog

Beneath Stars Long Extinct

Valve Job

The scalpel slides across his shaved chest
like a kitchen knife on top a quarter pound
of butter. I clamp back the folds, window
to a life. The breastbone gleams at me,
like a Thanksgiving bird's left over
from one of my mother's holiday meals;
my mother, who, above all in life,
wanted me in this business.

The osteotome makes quick work of splitting
Mr. Apgar's sternum, and there lies
the pericardium—translucent smoking-
jacket shrouding the heart—where our
goal reclines: a faulty aortic valve. It

doesn't look good, but we've been here
before: a lifetime of bacon, vodka,
tobacco and television. I don't judge,
just ask for the next tool necessary.
It's not our business why Mr. Apgar
did this to himself; a childhood
lacking love, the wrong wives (in serial),
and his own children's heartache. At fifty-
three, he's got more coming. We keep
working; slush the heart with ice
to cool things down; to buy us more time.

First Motor Vehicle Fatality in America

13 September 1899

Henry Hale Bliss, at Central Park West
and 74th Street, makes history.
At 68, Bliss, no stranger to chivalry,
disembarks a trolley car, and soon, life.
Well-tempered, a gentleman of fine breeding,
he turns, offering a hand to "a certain
Miss Lee." Mr. Bliss has avoided consumption,
smallpox, scarlet fever, and aliments taken
in association with ladies of ill-repute.

Arthur Smith, background unknown, early
Manhattan cabbie, allegedly swerves
to avoid hitting a truck. Miss Lee becomes
hysterical, her fingertips so close
to Henry Hale Bliss's, only a few thousand
moisture molecules of New York's late-
summer humidity between them before he
is rag doll-yanked away, his chest, his
grayed-head, crushed, thrown to cobblestones.

Perhaps Miss Lee was your mistress, Henry.
Perhaps you paid for kindness to a stranger
with your life. History has hid her from us.
We don't even know the fate of Arthur Smith
post-homicide charges. But you, Mr. Bliss,
you were first, and thus, remembered.
Number one in a line 30 million and growing.

Into First

Sixteen to the day, the first time
I legally sat in that front left seat.
Gripping the wheel—the roundness
of the world waiting—a hot black ribbon
laid below me, promising escape.
A fire-red Pinto, that defective
Detroit masterpiece famous
for exploding when rear-ended,
was mine, bought by countless
busboy dishes, and now, probably
compressed smaller than a mattress.

On my right for a change, my father
trying not to shout, ready to ride out
motion sickness, waited for me to find
the dual-foot, heel-toe sweet spot
combination. I eased out the clutch,
feeling for the right amount
of footpound push and release.

Then, the shudders,
the hesitation as she begged fuel
while commanded forward. Our
heads, practicing for whiplash,
rattled like insects in an epileptic
kid's jar. I restarted, tried again,
the stick forward into first,
the sweat-wet wheel and AM
radio all under my shaky sway.

That black ribbon and everywhere it
could take us waited, and behind,
an ugly childhood of inertia I left
as I slid the stick into second.
My father beside me tried to encourage,
not puke, his knuckles regaining color
as he watched me go.

Airline Stowaways

1947–2005

Countries were abandoned this way
sixty-nine known times. Home must be bad.
A precious quarter-sack of grain makes a guard
look away. Everything they know receding
on the hot tarmac-sprint to the taxiing plane.

Wet palms rise to the landing gear's steel.
They hoist themselves up, rubber rolling
faster on the cracked runway. Some return
home quicker than they wished as their grip
loosens in the rampening roar, the concrete

unforgiving. Those who ascend alive
sometimes lose a limb or two when
the hydraulic doors seal landing gear
safely. If not crushed to death as the tires

rotate inward, extreme cold and/or lack
of oxygen fixes odds against them.
Since commercial aviation started, they've gambled.
With fifteen known survivors, most lose.

On descent and approach to liberty—no
warning from the captain—the doors open;
tires rotate out. Most remaining fall, finally free,
their new homeland, large, rushing to greet them.

Exsection, Union Army, 1862

A bullet enters the upper-arm. You
don't bleed to death, no bayonet pierces
your side. There is, though, the long wait—
three days, maybe—in a hot milo field,
appropriately-named hardtack eaten,
canteen long dry. An orderly shows
to wrap the non-bleeding wound
with unsterile cloth before the feverish
cart ride to a school or house cum
field hospital. Your luck turns

here. Instead of adding your arm
to the pile of limbs outside, a surgeon
foregos the routine two-minute
amputation in favor of exsection.
With unwashed hands, he puts his fingers
into your wound, opening it to pull
shattered bone, lead fragments, and bits
of uniform. Anesthsia was first used
five years earlier, but there's none here.
The surgeon probes. Blank-eyed orderlies
pin you to the door lying on three barrels
faster than you could load your Springfield rifle.

You wake. Unlike many, your arm's still
attached. It hangs—because you're minus some bone
—useless but roaring like the glassblower's
glory hole back home in Maine. A cramped boxcar
ride north to Richmond, then Washington,

where there's a bed with not-too-dirty
sheets. A volunteer from Brooklyn
brings you licorice, reads to you,
as doctors wait for the staph infection
to win its battle. A blacksmith's fire burns
in your head, your arm, like cordwood, lies
never to hold your 15-year-old cousin-
fiancée again. In lucid moments you speak
to the volunteer, who writes
notes. Your mother opens his letter two
weeks too late. At the bottom it says, *As told
to Walt Whitman.*

Box of Ash

My friend Jim moved a graveyard.
One stiff he dug up was buried in 1974.
The cheap casket had collapsed,
allowing in grateful insects,
who cleaned the occupant to the bone.
When lifted out, he was held together
by his powder blue polyester leisure suit,
which looked like it had just come
from dry cleaning. I'm not going

in the ground, no.
A hole in the dirt? You're kidding,
right? This after my thigh's femoral artery
is (by law) opened, ten formaldehyde
pints pumped through, pushing my blood
out an incision in the other
thigh's femoral vein? You joke,

right? Then, the long subterranean wait
for worms, which will be much shorter
than waiting for the rapture
I am not now—nor will be then—
holding my breath for.

As if this insult in the earth wasn't enough,
they'll lay a stone saying what? A name,
some dates no one alive in eighty years
will remember? Maybe some words
unreadable two hundred years from now? *Not
a father, not beloved,* or *Inventor
of the New Jersey Backshaft Apparatus,* or *Whatever.*

This happens to everyone we know,
love and otherwise. We end. We are what
we leave behind, and the other way
around. Leisure suit, some writing,
a pat on the head in the sun: we drop
a memory—our tender footprint
on the earth—and then it's gone.

Half-brothers of the North Atlantic

Not such an unusual story. Willy H.,
Liverpool-born, 1911, comes to America
in '39 by way of Germany.
U.S. Navy enlistee, in '47
he loses his unfortunate surname
the way you lose a biting pet.

The not-so-usual part? Willy's
father, Alois Junior, had a well-
known half-brother. They shared a father
and a last name. This half-brother,
former trench soldier in the Great War,
stayed in Germany. Humiliated
by the Treaty of Versailles, by wheelbarrows
of cash to buy bread, he started talking,
then louder, singled out a few groups
supposedly responsible for everything,
set the box mustache back a millennia,
and, well, shit. You know the rest.

Not such an unusual story. Nephew Willy's
small town of Patchogue, Long Island.
Willy raises four sons: Alexander,
Louis, Howard, Brian. Good Americans,
by all accounts, they play baseball,
play army, graduate, settle
into middle-class ho-hum. None has children.
We can't help anything which came before.
We are everything—each arm-shot
into coatsleeve, all sighed syllables
—everything we leave behind.

My Father Rides with George Raft

not in 1931 or '43, but later. Later,
in 1955, when my father is sixteen,
and Westerns had eclipsed gangster
films. Hitchhiking to the Jersey
shore, the subbasement-black Cadillac
pulls up to Dad's porcelain thumb erect
in the July morning. He climbs
in, and the driver's familiar,
like the almost-remembered cousin
who didn't return from Korea.

Raft, always encouraging the myth
he was a gangster in real life, asks him about
broads, about hootch, about tough guys
in the neighborhood. This is before places
like Cambodia and Laos focus in my father's
consciousness. This is after Raft's popularity
slid and gangsters' romance receded, to return
like any tide. Dad looks at his driver, who wears
a black fedora and old-fashioned suit.
Rare-for-the-time air conditioning

keeps them cool. The man's voice is *refined,*
but a little rough, my father will tell his son
decades later. Dad doesn't think of arms
he'll one day bear for his country. He thinks
gangster, and that word trips it all into place.
Old movies. George Raft coolly flipping a half-dollar
in black and white. Glare washes the causeway
into Seaside Heights. The scene ends. My father
says *thank you*, his trigger finger the last
part of him touching the hot, black door.

The Longest Party

The One

Nina Voronoff, 7 February 1967 – 31 January 2000

Nina, I think of you, your yoga retreat
in Mexico. A week of muscles tightening
systematically across your body's
landscape: a grip behind the tibia,
a squeeze of quads against the femur.
There is the holding—hard, hard—
then the exhalation and release.

They call it a black box—what's searched
for in a frozen field, or lying
on drab sand far below waves—but it
isn't. It's bright orange, the color
of warning; a color yelling *here!*
The information it yields doesn't
help. We know you're gone. There's
no one to tell us the terrible seconds,
your galloping heart rate, your brown hair
blown back by changing cabin pressure.

We are better, sometimes, telling
each other the key information
unlocking seeming mysteries of trust
and emotional implosion. When we
heard the news, someone asked of your
boyfriend, *Do you think he told her?*
We wondered a collective half-second
and said, *yes.* You knew he was the one,
but he hadn't said the words we
need to hear from the right person.

Yes, Nina. We know he said it then.
As the fuselage's metal skin licked
the Pacific, perhaps even a grim
calm in his voice, he said it, your hand
gripping his like a mad dog's jaws.
Holding. Holding hard before
exhalation. Then one more squeeze
before the release, your fingers blooming
defiantly in the face of the greenhouse
door thrown open in January.

Telescope Closing

for a Manhattan resident, 11 September 2001

There are things I'll remember. I promise
you this. You lived in a city which never
became dark. Even if the thumbnail moon
was uncooperative, a roof of pale gray
clouds threw back our manmade light.

Remember our first date? You chose
the steakhouse and laughed when I
confessed I can't eat anything with a face.
But when you reached across your
sirloin to touch my hand, I knew it
was fine to be me; what I believed in.

There was our second date, the walk
up Park Avenue, over to Broadway, up,
up to my old neighborhood, across
from the natural history museum
where we relearned biology relates us all.

Then our third date. You showed
me the whispering gallery so few know:
the place I'll revisit alone, thinking all
the things unmentionable I wanted
to say that night, the things I couldn't
even whisper later, when you moved

above me, your outline rhythm-pivoting
until you were even faster than the taxi
headlights on the ceiling. What things
didn't I say afterward and why didn't I
keep us up so late we'd have overslept?

Sleep called me until your alarm did.
We walked to that place you got coffee
each morning, our goodbye not
long enough—yes, I should have brushed
your lips longer. Were you, too, thinking
that, the elevator taking you up, up alone,
over one-hundred stories? Yes, I'm selfish
enough to wish you thinking of me
as ceiling touched floor, then ceiling
to floor again and again, your world,
and mine, telescoping, closing
itself, shutting out all light.

Roadmaps to Work

Regarding professions, childhood
certainty was a lie. Fireman,
brain surgeon, astronaut; each
seemed desirable, even plausible
for ten minutes or a week
when I was five, nine, thirteen.

If, on dollars, I then wrote each thing
I could never imagine myself doing,
early retirement would be reality. Never
a wise investor, I find myself here,
grunting slightly as I slide Mrs. Horvath
into the dress her daughter chose.

The second arm is always harder,
as I do a combo lift-roll-insert
maneuver I like to think of as my own.
Barring exhumation, I'm the last one
who'll see her faded roadmap:
cesarean, appendectomy,
hernia, open-heart.

That evening, after dinner, my
girlfriend asks how work was. Slipping
her bank-job conservative suit jacket
from her shoulders, I kiss her neck,
my lips on her subtle pulse. Beneath
her blouse lies smooth-as-Sahara
skin. I fingertip-trace it all: her
beige clavicle, neck nape, fifth thoracic
vertebra, and I know I've found
the only profession I want.

When I reach her sacral triangle,
I can hear Mrs. Horvath's daughter
from earlier in the day. *She looks
beautiful. You do wonderful work.
You've done so well with what
you were given.*

Tell Them

Tell them, even if it's a lie, I went alone.
No family standing around my bed, no
paramedics working in vain. Tell them
I was the only child, still, mumbling
only to myself as the clock hands
strained for the ceiling.

Or say I was staring at the wall
thinking, *I'm glad I didn't repaint that.*
Tell them I was happier knowing I spent
those hours with a book, or walking
in October night rain, or just looking
out the window and saying that's right.

Tell them I went the way I wanted,
the way I dreamt of: holding her hand,
her hair sweeping my cheek as she whispered
something, in French, her native tongue
filling my ear: a phrase I didn't understand
but knew to mean everything was fine,
perfect, and always would be.

Requiem for Post-War Happiness

Lucky enough, I was, to see it.
Nothing. No worries. If my father
did his job, he'd have it forever,
and a pension after that. Our mothers
stayed at home, made us lunch,
gave us love. The cars had room
for backseat dance bands,
the bread whiter than our skin.
Crazy people were locked away—
our parents would not have been able
to spell *dysfunction*. Vietnam
was a French thing, a few fireworks,
nothing. What I remember best

were the bottles: thick, clear glass,
and taller than my skull.
My father put the empties in plastic
crates, carried them to a warehouse
where, by some American engineering
magic, they were sterilized and filled
to be brought home again.
The colors were a child's dream:
orange and purple and lemon lime.
Diet and *soda* hadn't yet been used
in the same sentence. Dad drank
cola; Mom, the root beer. Even
Grandpa—Gramps, who beat back
the Germans—drank Olde Tyme Cream
soda. We poured down that fructose

and went to the dentist. We
suckled all those empty calories
and returned for more. We
wanted to relive that initial tickle
of the fizz forever, which shot
through our heads like those months,
the miniscule bubbles which went
down so fast and delivered nothing.

Sergio's Tribe

In every generation of my ancestors, there's one.
Among factory workers, middle-management butt-
kissers, rubes who switched oxen-ass from sun-up
to barefoot, moonlit walks home, there was always
one: jobless. When we're nostalgic looking at their
grim, sepia stares and third-rate oil portraits we
may call them romantic. If feeling yet more
generous, we might say *that was Louie. He sketched*
Central Park. He was talented. In truth, I'm talking

the dreamers—slackers who worked mostly
in their minds. They shirked jobs, loved ones,
while dreaming better things for the world.
Sometimes they made lives around them richer:
a few tunes banged on drunken pianos, a homemade
valentine for a homely sweetheart, fresh flowers
from a field brought to the table in the only vase.

Their loved ones saw different. *Louie*
was lazy. And a louse. Shiftless, a card-cheat
with bad skin. These comments may survive
in a letter or two, but his sketches remain,
and thusly, Louie does moreso. Black sheep

I take after. They're best in their work,
such as it is, and I'm thankful their labor, their
paycheckless deviance from the norm. This one
strums a ukulele through the thirties,
that one bleeding bad watercolor mountains
on cheap, brittle paper. And there's Sergio,

whom I would've bought a drink or five.
He loved—so postcards tell us—to fish.
Not for money or the village families or even
a meal of his own. He did it for the blood's
pulse in his arms as he threw the net. He did it
to touch the writhe of life as he dragged it
aboard, struggling, gasping,
brilliant-shiny under the sun.

Family Dinner, No Truffles

My grandmother, her two sisters, and my great-
grandmother cooked for days. The food was fatty,
the refrigerators bulged, the oven heat stifling.

Peasants. The Old Country never had it so good,
and this was why they cooked and sauteed and baked
to excess. The relatives were making the pilgrimage

all the way from Bethlehem, Pennsylvania: two fat
women and their husbands, bringing greasy kielbasi,
obviously not nutritionally wise, but headed east.

The Depression left its mark on all of them,
and when they sat to eat, they grazed. The serving
bowls went round for thirds and fourths, the oil not

skimmed from the tops of soups, peas suffocated
in butter, the meat dead as shoeleather. The men
shoveled it in; chairs groaned under undue duress.

The women rose to clear the table and bring more,
everyone repeated, then they cleared the table again.
The men moved to the living room like bull elephants,

slow, weighted, snorting now and then. The women
teetered on orthopedic shoes, stacking empty plates,
stepping like tired buffalo, their dowager's humps

bulging beneath sail-sized dresses. The men,
belts open to accomodate their new loads, fell
asleep with baseball on television until

the women called them back for dessert. The
butter-loaded pastries insulted their hearts,
the sugar-loaded cookies kicked their pancreases.

They drank black coffee in effort to stay awake.
They ate like they never had before, year after year,
stuffing in place of what they couldn't give each other.

1951

The year Ethel and Julius Rosenberg were convicted,
the first atomic artillery-shell was fired, and a pulp
science fiction writer started a religion.

The year the Soviet Union successfully tested
a hydrogen bomb, "Doggie in the Window" played
on radios, and Americans bombed North Korean dams.

The year my mother took her turtle, Tommy,
into her father's garden, and there, among
twenty-inch zucchini and tomatoes so fat
their skins ripped, she removed Tommy's pill-
sized head at his not-as-hard-as-his-shell neck
with a stick on the black, life-giving soil to see
if he would still move, to investigate nature,
and to test limits of control.

Almost Enough

You're alone at an extended family
gathering. Cousins removed a few times,
nephews bearing no resemblance
to anyone surround you. No significant
other, no offspring you know of. Because
you never grew up, children of others
identify with you, and as snow tentatively
descends, you're employed as escort. Outside,
colors are beginning to surrender. The snow
is beautiful, for a time. Then your scrotum

tightens. You've had enough. You aim
for the door, but a camera is produced.
You should be here, someone says, pointing,
and you comply. Childless, you'll
become the forgotten cousin, nameless,
staring from a photo. The snow keeps
falling, muting colors, covering
everything. You've had enough. You turn
to enter someone's home,
where you know it's warm.

Anti-Darwinian

Frank Brugos Jr., 10 August 1945 – 29 October 2001

Not natural: a draft dodger so in love
with the trigger. What you did was unnatural,
always. Year after year, crouching in frozen
hedgerows, you waited for alpha males:
the big bucks, TV antenna-sized antlers
held aloft as they stepped—with almost
cigar-thin ankles—soundlessly into a field,
like recovery teams at a crashsite. Anti-

Darwinian: you culled out the best genes.
Not smart, not natural, you did it each frost-
covered season with grouse, partridge,
pheasant, rabbit, and almost anything else
which ran or flew. But there's some things
I want to know, Frank. When no god

sent you a check to keep the bills at bay,
did all those voiceless beings speak to you?
What did the chorus of beaks and muzzles
cry as you loaded that rifle one last time?
Were they silent as you put your mouth
on its business end? Each autumn

and winter dawn, as I'm unconscious
in my warm bed, I sleep well, Frank,
knowing this, you stupid bastard: deer
still break the woods. Their pool cue-thin
legs part brittle field grass—the frost licking
their black-polished hooves—as noses point
down corduroy rows of tan stubble. They see
what's before them, sniff, then move right on.

After Funerals

there's a party in honor of the stiff
who can't attend. His family pays
for it with a bit of his last paycheck.
In other words, he buys the booze,
cold cuts, the split atoms and cordwood
which run the lights and set the atmosphere.

Relatives and friends creep around,
say things like, *he looked good, don't*
you think? and *I wonder what they'll do*
with that leather jacket of his?

There's the former coworker, now sole
keeper of an affair's memories. There's
a family doctor (who failed), trying to merge
with the crowd. A priest gets sauced in the corner,
the dog looks for the one who walks him.
When they're full, talked tired, loaded

with memories, they leave. Disappear
like a landlord's smile, disassemble
as our molecules will when our lights go
out and the longest party finally breaks up.

Goodbyes

Late Again

It hurt badly. Not the same kind
of pain, but bad enough. Worse, even.

I came during off-hours; standing
alone at your bed, after visitors left—

your father's black scowl still lingering, your
mother's self-absorption wet on the floor.

Nurses grew to know me. As our days ticked
down, you'd get alert—witty, even—saying

*That one with the black hair—she's
your type. Find out when she's off-duty.* We

were holding hands and squeezed simultaneously.
If we were married, you'd be getting insurance dough,

you said, and we both gave weak smiles. I stood
through those nights, interns interrupting

my watch, your wrists refining themselves
to ivory dowel rods. You became smaller,

but I mentioned nothing. I was always too critical.
You woke once to say *The pain is, like,*

kneeling on me. I watched your chest,
your hips—all the parts of you I had held

and loved more than myself or anything I
could create—get smaller, distilled,

back to the little girl you were before we'd
met. You became the child I always wished

I could've protected. I failed you among
the tubes' lethargic drips, the whirring

machines; I failed you again, as I had failed
what was once us. Late. This, finally, hurt worse.

Choices, 1954

Before your mother, before even
my job on the Road Department,
there was Betty. My brother Jack
came back from Korea *sans legs*,
as they say. Dad built him
a ramp out back for the chair.
We didn't have anything back then;

there was nothing. The only choices
you had were to abstain or spin
the wheel of biologic chance.
Me and Betty spun that wheel
almost every afternoon, until
that Thursday after Algebra,
when she told me she was late,

and me, the fool, said *but
that was our last class*,
and Betty ran home, crying.
I went back to the house, thought
maybe I'd talk to Jack about girls
and such. He had dated the Rittner twin,
Homecoming Queen, '48. I found him

in the garage—Jack—his chair right
next to Dad's stepladder.
It couldn't have been long. He
was swaying just a bit, as if blown
by a baby's breath, moving from a height
where his toes would've almost
scraped the concrete.

World Without End

Along with the foliage this year,
you gave up. My ex-girlfriend,
your daughter, sits in the front row
without me, without a husband,
where neither you nor I can touch her.
I'm in the back, alone. Almost

my father-in-law, you lie
solo, a slight weight pulling
the corners of your mouth south,
perhaps the way you spent nights
thinking of me touching your daughter.
I never gave you the chance

for a wedding handshake, but did
slip her from under your roof. Today
the priest helps us say goodbye. There's
no talk of union, but lines about dust
and love and reward.
I didn't have the pleasure

of knowing John, the priest says
in a tone as tired as your given name.
Your life is represented in photos
among the flowers. This is the life
you chose. Your daughter and I chose
each other for awhile. When things—

including ourselves—weren't so great,
we stopped; probably should've stopped
chosing each other a few days earlier.
But you stuck it out: faithful to the end:
wife, job, and country. Later,
when you're suspended over the small

abyss to be your last home, the honor guard
folds your flag with great geometry: a symbol
you thought would last forever. The priest,
reading, says the three greatest things are faith,
hope, and love. We turn away, and I kiss
your daughter's forehead much the way you did.

Something Happens

Someone once said something
to somebody else, who distorted or tweaked it
a tad, then gave it to you: passed it on,
maybe twice, and it clicked. Those words made you
an opthamologist, or stayed your hand
when about to hit a child, or sent you the long way
to work one morning, avoiding a traffic fatality.

But something happens today. A guy says *au revoir!*,
steps off an interstate overpass, landing on a car
(small, blue), taking a family with him.
And so that someone is gone. Cameron or Walt
or Rasheed or Eddie has passed, but something
they said survives: an off-hand comment slipped
along, passed to you fourth-hand, years earlier.
These things happen.

And so, one morning, you take the long way
to work. You stop your car to let ducks
usher their young (fragile, puffy) across
the road. Children stand behind them,
careful not to cross, watching, wanting to learn this
and everything you've stopped questioning.
You, too, take it all in, oblivious of even a chance
of hearing sirens speeding on the interstate.

Hart, Weldon, John, and Me

Hart Crane off the stern of the *Orizaba*
and into the watercolor-blue Caribbean:
fish food.

Weldon Kees parks his car, walks the Golden
Gate above the bay chop to his last step:
fish food.

John Berryman accelerating off Washington
Avenue Bridge to smack the Minneapolis ice:
not fish food.

Then there's me—me, who wasn't supposed
to leave her amniotic ocean alive—and I'm
nineteen, thirty-five, even, and twenty meters
down in the most dense blue fog. I've glided
with pilot whales, looked into the maw
of whale sharks, skirted hammerhead schools.

The regulator's in my mouth and I'm smiling,
laughing at the doctors, bosses, the angry
young dope I was. My wetsuit's tight on my wrists,
and no one even notices the faint lines there
these years. Here's a gloved finger to Darwin
and all the gods. I'm breathing underwater, boys.

I'm breathing, and as I surface slowly—slowly
so nitrogen bubbles in my blood don't
expand faster than my hope—I salute you,

Hart. Here's to you, Weldon, and Johnny, too. I love the ascent's last four feet. The noise of equalization in your ears as pressure backs off is to die for.

Murmurs

The couple live together, work together:
he, a doctor, she a nurse, but these days
she runs the office, hounds delinquents,
fills out forms, makes claims. He still

practices, the cold metal disk to my chest,
reminds me to keep breathing. *Does your heart*
always beat this fast? Sounds like a little
tachycardia. I continue breathing. *Do you*

ever have anxiety? Fatigue? Panic attacks?
Yes. *Might be something simple, like mitral*
valve prolapse. We'll do more tests,
but start you on beta-blockers. Sometimes

there's side effects, like depression, unpleasant
dreams, and erectile dysfunction. I think
I'll skip beta-blockers, get another opinion.
Don't worry, you'll live, he says, smiling,

and I think how nice it is he's reminded me
of something else I had planned on
continuing to do. We leave the room
and he wordlessly hands my file to his wife.

At night, the stethoscope lies curled
on his dresser, its cold, sensitive
instrument pointed toward the bed,
listening for something. Anything.

Untitled

is not a good way to start. The title
is the flight plan, the primer, the road sign
telling us what to expect. You worked
hard on this. It deserves a name.

It—the title—can convey information
whole sentences can't. It can do little,
or even harm your verse, so be careful.
You can do damage here, like naming

a son John Jr.: unimaginative, twice,
or a played-out daughter's name:
Jane, Kate, or Alice. Let's face it:
we're making what consumers won't buy.

Where's the glitz? Hawk it! Let's sell
this mother. Hopefully you worked hard.
It deserves a name, as does anything you
brought into this world from nothing.

Guitar Show

The sky offers us what we can barely call rain:
a thin mist, the occassional droplet added
as an apology. I get in line with the others, all
of whom can be summed up in two groups.
There's those who've given up: former rock
and rollers who now own homes, short hair, children.
They work in offices, study prospecti, worry
about merging. Then there's the others:

the guys who hang on, year after year, no
day job, no wife (who would have them?),
a few gigs a week, at best, their lower backs
reminding them of the years as they hoist
amplifers into trucks with bald tires.
These are the men I like. Children in so many
ways, they wait in line to see both the latest
models and guitars from the glory days
of rock. I move among them, the frizzed-out,
tired hair thinning on top, sunglasses indoors,
the hackneyed licks flailed out on new six strings
they can't afford. Overhearing their talk, it all
takes shape. Some give lessons, some pickup
a few hours labor as a carpenter's assistant
from a younger brother too kind to say no.
They talk of opening for this act and that singer
before the lines were cut into their foreheads
like tree rings. They miss vinyl, guitars
stolen over the years, and the contract
they were let go from before they recorded.

When I've seen and heard enough, the sky
gives us something more respectable. Dime-
sized drops explode as I get into the car.
Leaving this behind, pulling onto the highway,
I merge into a funeral motorcade. Switching
my lights on, I ride a string of mourners,
the decay of some notes in the distance fading.

Ex-girlfriends' Friends' Ex-boyfriends

We, guys, are over. Our runs done,
and when our ex-girlfriends are bored
or tired or just need something
to complain of, we're remembered,
and not well. The equation

is simple: we're not in their
present lives equals
we left them or they dumped us equals
bitterness, equals
shit list. Our dumbest hopes,
private fears, and sublime secrets
are passed around like bags of stale
chips. Our low points are compared: cheap,
unfaithful, unresponsive, non-
committal, selfish, sloth-like
on the sofa. We may see

each other on streets of cities
we haven't lived in with our old
loves. If you recognize me, nod,
but don't stop. We can't exchange
hellos without remembered names.
We're criminals who broke hearts—
our penis sizes compared
for squeals on some premenstrual
meltdown-moody night—and we
should observe the silent codes
of thieves of time, of criminals
between sentences. We'll glance with
the knowing, quiet look of humbly
rehabilitated men on parole.

Chart into Midlife Straits

Your girlfriend's underwear has less
surface area than a square of toilet paper.
You love her for this, among other things,
but this is way up there. Then things change.
Days leave you as you left other women:
unconsciously or without a word or with it
being no one's fault. Days do what they want.

Your heart—which got you into this—
pumps less efficiently, your hairline
on the run for the back of your head.
You play certain parts of your skeletal
system like percussion instruments,
and bathroom trips bring more
pleasure than you ever imagined.
Surgeons cut things out; you keep
going. Jar lids are tighter. Your
own underwear gets larger even if
your waistline doesn't. Suits aren't
so bad. Your life's soundtrack plays
just fine as instrumentals. Your
parents' faces only clear in photos,
your friends reproduce with alarming
regularity, but you're free, wifeless,

looking back across temporal plains
for the child you weren't as a boy.
Better than the alternative, you
cast off, your years lashed together

as a raft, your massive underwear a sail
for the breezes of old age, eyes fixed
on the razored horizon for a hint
of the man they told you you'd be.

Temporal Men

Perhaps better nameless, the men
who came before me outlasted
my relationships with women
we shared. First names remind me
of holiday snapshot dopey grins, voicemail,
and tales of unions' downslopes.

As past tense recollections, I knew
men long gone emotionally, but still
visiting us on the answering machine.
Their ghosts watched us in a bed
they once helped warm. Men with regrets,
men with new wives, and men with both.

Today, a guy says, *I'm Jeff. I'll
be your waiter.* Is he the Jeff
sharing thoughts of the same
woman's throaty moan? What's certain
is our waking miles apart
in common moonless blackness, aware

unconfronted ache brings union
to us all: our voices' timber,
who we are—even our names,
once whispered among infinite
yeses—will someday
animate no memories.

Service

The biggest Catholic church in town
was so poor there was no church.
The gymnasium of the hideous, mid-century
architecture parochial school served Sundays
for the faithful. No mahogany pews:
folding metal chairs (with folding padded
knee stools) were lined up more rigid
than our hungover fathers. To the basketball
court preached the other Fathers, His
employees, paid marginally with our dads'
suburban salaries via collection baskets.

When, mid-semester, a high school girl
stopped showing up Sunday mornings,
it was said she decided to attend private
school out of state. When the wife-beater's wife
couldn't take anymore and her divorce
came through, she was asked to come
to Saturday night services only,
then not at all. Altar boys, entrusted
with blood and body paid penance in silence.

The faithful stood and knelt and sat and said
the words on cue, moving like well-lubed
machinery. Usually, a priest asked to pray
the Asian communists to death, or at least
make them see the light so no more
suburban sons would be sacrificed.
Those same sons' mothers and fathers
marched up the foul lines, aimed their
tongues, took the cracker, a hit of grape juice,
and sat down until told to do the next good thing.

Elementary School Librarian

Mrs. Harkins, even your name was harsh.
What made you this way? Was it some late-
19th century book on child rearing
your parents read? Perhaps you received
the business end of it: a razor strop
to break the will of the curious child.

You tried to break ours by starting with our
names, the first word we learned, the first
word we wrote. You made up your own
pronunciations: *Doughty* was *Dockerty*,
Nuzzi became *Nootsy*. You smacked
our fingers when we didn't turn pages
the way you liked, until some parent's lawyer
reminded you corporal punishment was dead.

Harkins, you made fun of the way some
of us spoke. You did this before our classmates.
You did this wearing tight leather skirts
and knee-high leather boots. Our young
teachers rolled their eyes at your outfits
when you weren't looking, maybe imagining
a catonine tail hanging from your bedroom
doorknob, your husband ballgagged
and bound over the ottoman. All right,

all right, I digress. Harkins, you were crazy.
Unfit to be near children, let alone teach
them to love books. You were old then,

so you're dead or drooling in some (poorly,
I hope) state-run facility, safely tucked away
from youth. The last time I saw you
was high school, long out of your grasp.
Instantly my friend gave you the finger.
I didn't marvel his bravery or even your
face's shock. I remember how straight
that finger was. Straighter than any book spine,
firmer than any hardcover. It rose above all,
becoming the tallest point in our lowbrow
town. It pointed the only way left to go.

Heartworm and the Space Behind

From the car, the dog—Miss Sue—
watches the man carry long things
into the field. One she knows, one
she doesn't. Miss Sue will not be here
much longer, but she's happy. She leaps
from the car, excited to be in the field.
Her tail cuts the space she leaves behind,
but her leg hurts where she's bitten it
to relieve discomfort there—
irritation connected to something
burrowing deeper inside her, something

she doesn't feel. The man crouches
and Miss Sue runs to him. He removes
her collar, which almost never happens.
She circles, following the exponentially
increasing scents, smelling the alive things
life presents her in this moment.
The man works one long tool he's brought,
opening the ground. Miss Sue sniffs
his progress, but the hole is uninteresting.
She smells the oiled blued steel
of the other tool

and is ready to find, freeze, and point.
Then the blast will crack. She knows
it's then safe to retrieve the bird
or smaller mammal who did not
know what was coming fast.

Nine Months

New Love Versus Viral Load

Of the one I love, I'll say this: I'm so afraid.
I was a sickly child, my resistance is still weak.
Although not death, there's still danger in getting laid.
What's the gamble's cost for the union of our physiques?

I was a sickly child, my resistance is still weak.
Open sores and viral shedding is how this may turn out.
What's the gamble's cost of the union of our physiques?
But holy shit! Look at her body, her eyes, how her lips pout.

Open sores and viral shedding is how this may turn out.
This is love, not sex. In both, our heads don't think right.
But holy shit! Look at her body, her eyes, how her lips pout.
Think of all those microscopic bastards ready to smite.

Latex and drugs are iffy in their protection of my blood.
Although not death, there's still danger in getting laid.
It hurts to look at her, like a valley before the flood.
Of the one I love, I'll say this: I'm so afraid.

Kissing

Your two orbicularis oris muscles
contracted, pushed forward, at least
at first, to meet orbicularis oris
muscles doing likewise, attached
to someone hopefully feeling
earnest, bent upon as you.

The mouth. The mouth is the thing;
the aperture through which we enter
that which keeps us going; i.e., fuel.
You'd fast a week—sell an organ, even—
to mirror your lips to those surrounding
the voice whose name you love to say.

If things are going as planned—
schemed in minute millimeter detail
while driving, dreaming, while
kissing someone else; i.e., the wrong
person—you get more than a kiss-
grandma-goodbye-kiss. Two pairs

of lips open and something expands
in your vitals. Perhaps it's your
cynicism pushed out, falling away,
maybe making abdominal room
for trust someone offers as they slip
it to you just ahead of their tongue.

Or it's that unspeakable thing swelling
in you, right person-requited this time:
that thing you're so reluctant to own
after a life of rentals, of homelessness
even. You build it close-eyed; foundation
laid by sweet, scrupulous labor of your lips.

In Lieu of Work

Imagine this. I put some words on a piece of paper.
They may say I miss the insular rings of color
in your irises, or how my bed without you is cold
as an elected official's handshake, or that I can't
imagine a world ignorant of your smile. The words
are put on paper when I'm supposed to be working,
earning dollars: those things ultimately enabling
me more time with you. My lips press just below my
signature for luck before sealing it inside
another piece of paper. I put a stamp on
the outside, then another just to make sure it will find
you. I write your address—oh, this is bad; even your street
name makes me sigh—in black pen, hoping the postal worker's
heart will jerk quicker when he sees your name. With
reluctance, I drop it into a dark mailbox to lie
among oppressive bills, too-thin checks, greeting cards
to unvisited Aunt Vivian, where I know its own
pale light will leak from corners of the envelope
and suffragettes, inventors, even deceased
crooners on stamps will sigh with envy.

You may come home that day from work: yoga instruction,
the grunts of suburban housewives still sounding in
your slender ear. Among the bills, the advertisements,
the yoga magazines ("keep your spine aligned with this
axis in a proper downward dog pose"), you'll find my
thin white rectangle, my black handwriting calling your
name. You'll open it and know I'm hooked, wriggling as if
pulled from a life I can't even recall. You'll know I'm then—

that moment—thinking of you, my hips not plumb as I
lean a bit northeast toward you until the last of my
resistance, my self-control is gone, and I'm in my car.
Moving never fast enough, I'm parking under those trees
where birds nudge each other, preparing their metabolized
berries and insects. I'm skipping up the steps like a school-
girl. I wave to the neighborhood widow, give the homeless
guy all my change. I carefully step around the ant hill,
even sparing every dedicated drone, working, earning
for his queen. I take a half-breath, hold it—your mailbox
open, waiting for more—and ring the glowing bell.

In Training

I went four years with a woman, once—
a phrase I say not unlike going four
rounds with a welter weight owning
a vicious straight right. I stepped out
of the ring a little addled, but okay.

I went four weeks with you before
I wanted to make it legal. Okay,
not too fucking legal, as in with child,
but I'm coming around. I'm coming
around to that, even. I'm bobbing

and jabbing, baby. But not just me!
We've got to train, comrade. This
is physical, I tell you. And I mean
train. No fruity yoga. I'm talking
sweat. Together. You and me.

We'll bob. Each of us will go down.
This is toning up for the big
bout. We'll do it hard, multiple
times, all day. You notice how I
left hand-hold you when we practice:

cupping your most graceful curve:
your sacrum. I'm getting you in shape.
My right hand's been on your belly
just south your navel. Feel my warm palm
pressed here as you say *yeah. Yes. Yes.*

The energy's present, but not quite. We're
doing it; getting there. I'll touch it
each time we train. It's happening, baby,
I'm feeling it right here, champ—under
my palm. Our win. Our future. Our prize.

Wedding Date

Autumn's here; a time no couple without
a gun to their backs get married.
I open thank you notes containing
comments by new Misters and Missuses.
They're back from Bali or the Greek Isles
and want to see us, have photos
to share of how happy we were
on their special day.

We set a record. No new couple attended
as many weddings in their first four months.
After our lengthy, separate searches,
what better dates could we go on? We
had what couples should be forced to prove
on their wedding day. We left witnesses—
nieces and baby half-brothers
remember us as the ones who kissed a lot.

Parents, pale from caterer bills, saw it
and congratulated us. Brides and grooms
received us with envy. On their day
it shone from within us, contagiously:
the groomsmen slipping you phone
numbers on your way to the ladies room,
the maid of honor cornering me
at the coat check. We were the ones

who left banquet halls to find sofas
where we kissed the way new husbands and wives

wanted to. The open bars, the rubber
cordon bleu chicken, the Caucasian
two-step, and you: perfect. I loved it all,
beaming during slow dances more
than the spinster aunts. The bands butchered
songs, children cried to go home. Dreaming

like a schoolgirl, I wanted it
to be us up there, the knives against
stemware until we'd lean together,
our lips locking amid cheers.
Honeymoon done, a blind turn approached.
We became our parents before our time.
We did it without gown or limo; we did it
without a single I do. Autumn's here.

I come to bed in darkness, and though I'm
silent with wonder, your earplugs are in.
The day uncoils from my body
as I ready myself for dreams
of tropics, of ceremony, of old friends
lined up to wish us well. You don't
move, your black sleep mask keeping
out any light which may enter our space.

Rear-ended

Each day opened before me
under your eyes' brightness.
Warmed, I then faced evenings
with you as like-things do,
protecting themselves against
night's chill: rose petals, your
white sheets, our limbs folded
together fiercely close—
closer—until there was chance
for nothing between us
which shouldn't have been there.

Now, as snow surrounds my car,
keeping me at your side for the duration,
I think of the accident we witnessed:
the old couple on an undisturbed vector
before the unseen impact from behind.
One passive moment's stare ahead
in ignorant bliss; the jolt
into disbelief as the present
overtook, spinning them—
leaving even the air between them
astonished at the unpredicted change.

True East

Hard as silverware, your penis points
the way out of bed, a compass needle
heading true east. Your girlfriend's eyes
move behind her lids, one earring lying
on your pillow, divorced. Rising, you leave
the bed as you did your childhood days:
splayed behind you, unordered, in chaos.

Washing, the mirror reminds you of your
parents, those often-striking air traffic controllers,
whose own faulty bearings gave you fouled-up
coordinates, mistaken headings over distant airfields
where safe childhoods waited on the ground.

Your penis subdued now like an unruly child calmed,
you dress near the bed. Your girlfriend's eyes
slide behind her lids, search for offspring.
You bend to kiss her gently-creased forehead.
From her lips, frozen open the width of a baby's
tiniest toe, you swear you can hear words leaking out.
Why? Why won't you give me any children?

Notes for Second Summer

Spring trips over itself in coming
this year. I'm counting on it,
expecting it, unlike the way
you entered my life. Summer
will make it, too, our backs in T-
shirts stuck to car seats.

Rocks I carried you from the Pacific
still sit, arranged Zen-like, cold, waiting
your touch; the ottoman a dumb monument.
Nearby, your vacant sofa continues
its vigil. All that crushed velvet—
where I once wept realizing I'd found
you—waiting, as you sleep in the room
just above it, perhaps alone.

Not far, I'll sit on my own sofa,
the day's heat burning off, the wet
breath of deciduous trees leaking
into my window. I'll write through
the night, as I did last summer,
fall and winter on your sofa,
you sleeping just above me.

This summer will be hard. I'll be thin,
the pounds of cold-month sadness slipping off
like layers of clothes. I'll be thin; women
will look. I may touch their necks, smell
their hair. Even the nights' middles will be hot,
but something in me—right here—will sit
cold, waiting. Notes will be made in dim light.

Your sofa will be empty, patient. Even now
I miss it terribly—the cushions, tense
with ripeness; space over it barely
breathing for lack of passion.

The Closest

Your bed is the easiest to remember.
The boxspring too small for the frame,
we never knew when it would collapse.
Without warning it dropped away beneath
us, as did the one great thing we held
here, below the breastbone for each other.

The mattress was its own nightmare.
Canoe-like, we arose hammered, our
spines with aches reminding us
of past loves, residuals of failed promises.

No matter how early in the morning
I'd finally come to bed, you were there,
your supple, gorgeous—yes, gorgeous—
limbs waiting for me to double
immediately behind you until our
chests rose and fell in unison on the same sea.

You'd leave me unconscious in mornings.
I'd wake there in your room—your most
private space—where you trusted me.
I made that bed, darling. I did. Alone.

I did it with a care I don't have for my
own life. The sheets and covers military-
tight, the flat pillows laid at the head,
the frilly ones over them. The small,
decorative pillow placed between those,
balanced on a corner. Last, the beaded
shawl spread tightly, covering up
the place we were closest.

Love and Otherwise

Hazel Address

There's faintest hints of crow's feet
streaming back from your hazel glances.
These are the places I'd like to be: climbing
the minute ridges, seeing what you
see, the way you do. I want to be here,
where, as we slip into those ages in which
our parents seemed impossibly old, our
faces begin to betray the number of years
we've spent looking for our mates.

I want to make my camp here, my home.
I'll risk what comes with lying in your
lowlands: a flash flood of tears,
the occasional harsh rubs of love,
inflammations which come and go
with mistakes we make: the welts
of life. It would be good for me:
the peasant, homesteading near your
cosmopolitan smile, your refined palate.
I'll cook over an open fire, my things
beneath a quarter moon. I'll be a sooner,
a claim-jumper. I'll be the squatter,
ever watchful of what comes next:
a cooling exhalation, a sigh, a wicked
grin tightening our whole landscape.

Leavening Agents

Because your people believed
in a supernatural being
different from the one my people
bowed—in grief, not reverence—their heads
to, we're in this mess.

Way back, my people threw in their lot
with that happy group who branded
themselves with a guy nailed
to a piece of wood. Good logo.

Kneeling. Penitence. Abstinence. Guilt.
Fun, fun. Joy.

Your people, way back, thought something
a better bet: bitter herbs and fasting
to emulate suffering of others
long since turned to dust.

Smiting. Scattering. Atonement. Guilt.
Yeah. Nice. Great.

And now, my love, you and I: different
tribes. Both Westernized worships, but far
enough apart to cause disappointment,
distrust, dual wedding.
If there's kids, yes, fine, sure. We'll raise

them to think, to question. They'll know
the dolt enroute to his factory job
every pre-dawn and the yak-herder
on starlit steppes and the sonambulist

body-washer share the same thing.
Our children will rejoice knowing they're all

our people: as they leave their loves
sleeping safely, as they pray
for rain, as they walk into blinding,
thawing sun.

Now come here and kiss me, for chrissakes.

Passing

Following the ribbon of red taillights,
a stream of white ones coming at my left,
on the drive to touch the only woman
I've wanted to marry. The doe leaps

from my right to left. Despite black ice,
I brake in time. Headlights highlight her
taught muscles tapering to thin sticks.
She bounds into the other lane, and I pass

the space where she was last whole.
Then, I'm in a warm home, my love's
face a tangible prayer in my hands.
Her eyes are beige, and I close my own

before kissing. I put everything
into that kiss: I want this to work.
In the darkness I see what I missed
driving, but heard after passing:

someone else's brakes barking
and the busting of solid things
the naive assume will last.

After Almost Marrying a Woman With Your Name

...for whatever we lose (like a you or a me)
it's always ourselves we find in the sea.
— E.E. Cummings

The ocean's briny wilderness continues
with or without me. This is why I dive.
Sucking from the regulator, marine life
I can't speak to swims through sunken enterprises.

The hours were yours. My hours, yours too.
From the first day of fifth grade, you wanted nothing
from me. I looked, sighed—did so daily until high
school graduation, a thin fog between us always.

A humpback whale rolls on its side—black eye
softball-sized—and I hang in her gaze.
Neither of us blink, two mammals underwater,
one where he shouldn't be. I want to touch her,
remove a barnacle proving she's here.

Our semesters were yours. I watched your blond hair
brown, hormones exploding
in their insane race to make us adults.
You clutched your cum laude diploma. I loved
and didn't, gave and got, gave and didn't get.

Stunned by all she is, I can't reach out.
Massive pectoral flipper a white sheet
I want to wrap myself beneath, she pushes
away, her sublime tail in subtle motion,
and I lose her to the ultramarine.

Our years have been your own. You were married,
then not. You told me this at our reunions: ten,
then twenty years. And the career: I picture you
defending, pouring over precedents, settlements.
You told me of your boyfriend. You turned, walked.

Climbing the dive boat's stern ladder, something
within me gives way. I fall. My weighted
tank, my mask, pulls me faster, back
into the blue. I reenter that immense thing
I can't help but love.

Maps of Time

Somewhere south, a woman you loved
extrudes a pasty-headed child
between thighs once meaning the world
to you. Half-her, half- the guy crouching
near her neck—telling her, *breathe honey,*
breathe—it's not the child you once
thought you'd witness drawing its first
astonished breath.

Somewhere west, a woman you loved
stops a cauterwaul by placing
her left nipple in a dime-sized
mouth—a nipple near where you once
laid your own head; a place above
a heart you had held wholly.

You curl into the childless
woman drawing long, identical
breaths, her perfect curves unchanged
by all you've given her through tonight.
Your body echoes her pose, your
head on her dark hair. You try not
to wake her, you don't disturb.
You close your eyes, breathe carefully,
hoping to upset nothing here.

Baby

Sometimes it's me on top of a woman,
the lights mercifully dim, hiding something
proving I'm slipping fast, ass-first, in the mud-
slide downward to middle-age. My hand
blind in her blond hair, her ear almost in my
mouth when I sluice two syllables into her: *baby,*

beaten in time with my staccato pulse.
Sometimes it's me working vernacular popular
before I was born: *this mortgage is killing me,*
baby. Next, I'll be calling men cats because,
well, it just, like, sounds groovy, baby.
Sometimes it's me hearing my girlfriend
deliver the one-two combination of what she
needs from me to become whole: babies.

I know it best as me, the only child,
the baby, always. I know it when I'm
supposed to be a man doing things men do:
a valve job, dry wall work, underwater welding,
a good hunter-gatherer, but before starting
these jobs, I feel what I am
unrolling up my spine like a father's belt
on my lilly-white back: baby.

Notes Concerning the Universal Truth

As you kneel to tie your shoe
the man you should marry
strolls by in no hurry to his
psychotic girlfriend, his eye
looking for new love. It happens

like this. Your friend passes
a bottle of water as you merge
too quickly, setting in motion
a nine car pileup, killing a researcher
who, seconds before, made mental
notes on a correct theory curing
cancer, and you drive away,
oblivious, talking of nothing,
thirsty for more.

This is it: a world of chance.
Events in motion spiraling around
us, buffeted by our half-hearted
backhanded comments, gestures,
and inertia. Not a place to understand,
not a place inviting the planning
of next year, but we dredge ourselves
from the mattress each morning
and tread water to work.

Sometimes it's for the better,
like when on line at the bank.
You handicap the pensioners, judge

numbers of their checks, divide
by speed of the tellers, then choose
a queue. Someone blows their nose
an extra time, someone's car
didn't start on first try, and it
works: you step to the window

of the woman with car crash-causing lips,
eyes which make even myopic men linger,
and her smile says *now*; it is the smile of *here*.
You place your checks on her counter, give her all
you have, and say *walk me through this, please.*

Minor Rock Star Confessions

This was not high art. This was before bands
paid to play clubs; when you could smoke indoors.
I teased a six-string, cauterwalled, and lost
hearing. Women came: underage drinkers

and late thirties women with babysitters
watching results of recently-ended marriages.
We played songs of death, of love—
often the same thing—maybe one

about fast cars thrown in.
The boys' heads became broken
metronomes as drinks marked hours.
They mouthed words to our most-loved songs,

hooted on cue for the solos.
In that dark field of cobalt smoke traversed
the need to connect between each pair
of black eyes and mine—the common

thing we strangers were there for.
Later, sweaty ladies waited for my signature,
handshake, posed photo: each one breaking
things in me to various degrees.

This was back, back when our lungs
filtered air until the last floor-mopper
went home and only dawn's
dull blade cleared the last smoke.

Nights, they leaned forward, lips
puckered around a paper
cylinder holding dried leaves. I'd stick
out a flame in the darkened booth,

draw them in. I took my guitars home
alone. I made them cry in my smokeless
apartment while imagining all those eyes on me.
It was the thing I intended to happen.

Poopie Head

is the term my niece uses for people
who don't acquiesce. It's jargon
of choice among the preschool set,
apparently. Poopie head playmates
and babysitters and plenty of poopie head
teachers on the way, little Emily.

Poopie head coaches and backstabbing
ex-best friends. Vapid teen idols
and genetic freak models with poopie head bodies.
Prom date, virginity-taker, noncommittal fiances,
ex-husband: poopie heads. Poopie head
landlords, preachers, and wedding reception
caterers. Midlevel managers
maintaining poopie head glass ceilings.
Married men, non-vasectomied Internet dating men.
Poopie head ombudsmen, whistling
construction workers, and don't forget
the big one: poopie head President.

Emily, I like your melding of our waste—what's left
over from fuel we put in ourselves—with our minds:
our beings. No, Emily, there's nothing wrong
with you. All the millions of biologic happenings
inside you each night ensuring your eyes open
every morning: perfect. It's the others,
Emily. It's them. Poopie heads, all.

Sweet

Sweet, because—for once—I wasn't looking
for love. That's when it happened:
you saw me in the airport; I hadn't given
you a first glance. Sweet we shared
a tropical destination, and sweeter
that once there, by chance, I sat at your
communal table. Sweetly you said
we were from the same city, and again,
sweet the way something amber in you
spread across said table,
like tectonic plates, like spearmint candy
in a bankrupt mouth. Then the easy idle
of the vacation week at your side:
our bodies burning and browning, white
sand in your black hair, the syrupy booze
which fueled our dancing each night.
Sweeter how you offered to share a cab
from the airport into our city.
Tonight, I picture you in your room.
Think how my beach-kisses tasted:
spiked pineapple juice, urgent stubble.
Beyond everything rational, you'll think
of me as you taste them again
in near-blackness with your lover.

Human Papilloma Virus

Spring's first day vibrating like a razor
above the thigh of a girl who hates herself,
I serve the woman I love breakfast on the terrace.
My eggs radiate with the sun, imported

jam for the toast. I'm scoring points, home run
after home run. She's talking of me meeting her folks.
The mimosa is sublime, Bessie Smith sings
about some bastard, and my love glances over

the top of *The New York Times*, now and then, just
for my eyes. The phone rings, and I'm feeling
generous, so I answer. My ex- blurts
she's been to a doctor. She's got it and I'm

probably a carrier because she's been with no one
else, and to watch for warts, and in longshot cases,
cancer of the penis, and to have a good day, bastard.
I hang up, tell my love it was just work.

My grandfather, who was a bastard literally
and personally, was probably a carrier,
but his son-in-law most likely wasn't. My father
had warts on his feet he said came

from playing catcher in the majors, but science
tells us are from some other virus. Dad, frighteningly
young those spring afternoon games, never
a bastard, crouching low to the earth, the balls

of his feet dug in it. Stadiums poised to erupt
if he caught or failed; China-white hands in front
of him, waiting for that southpaw bastard to fire
his vicious curve, waiting to catch it. Waiting

for me to issue forth from his insanely young
wife, who waited at home, dreaming I'd grow into
a fine young man batting .430, not sleeping around.
A man completely different than her father, that bastard.

Strata Marginalia

On an October Thursday a mother
climbed down a tree. Stupified neighbors
watched her stand on hind legs to see
over the tallest grass. This enabled
predator evasion, and helped find
new trees to climb. It ensured survival,
thus her descendants, in turn, did it
again, and more, becoming bipedal.

No mystery. With their front limbs off
the ground they got the hang of stones-as-tools,
which increased cranial size. This means
instead of preening sand fleas from my mate,
I can play the fucking guitar. It
also means the chapter human will be
marginalia in Earth's strata:

an unsightly anomaly
of petroleum-based plastics, asphalt,
and disposable diapers packed between
sandstone and shale. Whatever evolves from us
or whoever lands here from some planet
we dream of, will have intelligence
evident; will exist owing to its
own design. All the less-sharp, faultily-
built, and not-too-lucky natives of this
worried marble will be over, dust, not
even an echo, along with their
music and dreams; their fashion and gods.

Brownian Motion

It's a tough job, this thing of coming together,
then the leavings. Our hopes rise and recede
in cages of our ribs as each new love steps
to shade we provide. Marseilles to the Cape
of Good Hope, West Memphis to Brisbane.

It's pretty much the same everywhere.
Average ejaculatory speed is 28 miles per hour
(45 kph). We rush our lives to get here,
these few seconds, over and over, decades on
and on, where we're unself-conscious, blissful, dumb.

Headlights on the ceiling remind us
an entire involuntary network's out there,
moving without our command, yet bringing
us the things we can't do without; things
preventing us from withering alone:

wine, eyeliner, shoe lifts. Once entering
the vagina, sperm take five minutes
to cross six inches of love's terrain to the cervix.
That's .0011 miles per hour, and *that* makes
sense. We run to love—doing pushups while waiting

for the phone, back-waxing, cleaning compulsively—
whatever. Then it's here, for a bit, and we're
breathing hard until we're sated, granted-taking, fat.
And across every map there's the arrhythmic
flutters—unseen sea tides expanding, and not—

in countless chests. There's the hope it'll last,
and it won't, because we don't. It's a job
of millimeters and seconds, of random chance.
It's eyes locked with a stranger in a packed
subway car. It is the blessed tension
until the lights flicker out.

Biographical Note

Ron Egatz has worked as a bartender, creative director, forklift operator, guitarist, security guard, college English teacher, cab driver, actor, typesetter, summons server, director of commercials and IT consultant. He now runs Camber Press, Inc. Winner of the *Glimmer Train* Poetry Open and the Greenburgh Poetry Award, Egatz lives in a loft on the Hudson River while missing Paris.